Mystical Weather #1

Mystical Weather #1

Jeremy Garcia

Jeremy C. A. Garcia

Mystical Weather
#1
By Jeremy. C. A. Garcia

Contents

Question Authority

Can you see just like the king?
Perfect in self, knowing what to dance to
Collaborate in life to sing
The works of the enemy to prance to
Settle for the beauty
Exchange your wicked garden to the ones that knew of he
All the time
My head is spinning
Looking for the temple
The fat is thinning
Praying is able
Can you see like the king?
Eye love eye
Everlasting ring
Living around a harden lie
Spend you chime in sin
Away from the lord with a grin
Could you see? Be able to be in peace while you are free
Would you see? The consciousness of the rightful law and let it be
Can you see like the king?

The Lighter

Run! Soldiers are the headline of the time
Be aware! Sin in death being the shine
Won't I not be a included in the rhyme
Come forth the Creator from my whine
Said prepare for the king's return in stable dance of the music surrounding
Sin, it's heart loud, it's pounding
In calm yet overshock from the world we all live in
I'm to be a light overlooked from the world we all give in
Run to God
Be aware of the enemy
It has the same rod
Keep faith in God
While War is the light of Life.

Lovely Thought

Whispers allowing the sun shine
Gossip making it rain
Her kiss tenders my soul
Shouts make the night appear
Cursing in screams making the tornadoes
Her hugs keep me safe in soften touch
Time to move on in life
Past dances loving puppy wife
Ballin' sexual memory sharp as a knife
Conversations of life
Insanity makes the weather
Sanity in prison calms the tide
Her name stables my soul
Offense appear in danger
Defense happens in danger
Her existence has enlightened my spirit
Time a'comin' along with life
Past dances loving puppy wife
Ballin' sexual memory sharp as a knife
Conversations of life.

Social Media

That group has no care
Only they have pride
For making a platform where you need to be beware
In the dark where sinners hide
Preacher directs no sin with the platform
Family knows suicide as a movie
Group gives no attention of that harm
Yet it's made from their hands that grooves we
A gathering of caring cry in protest
Shines the group beauty sleep
Interruption during the taking of the test
Students sin being apart from God in too deep
The group of students are the head of a platform that sins with having no care only being prideful.

The One Ignites War

She dances for the blind ruler
He takes orders from the blind ruler
Harden worry from the departed
Being able to attend with a blind eye
Knowing the danger, makes the prayer strong in the hands of the
hearted
In being able to eat from grind rye
Directs the lessons of the path of the true creator

Once

Wicked I was
Golden in sin
Thicker the puss
Smolder wicked grin
In chains without regret
Wise screams stop
Voices shine the sinful act
Self-thought beats the heart of guilt
I'm sorry without regret
Surprise to continue life's hop
Voices dim from meds in the sinful compact
Learn my lesson,
growing from the confession,
in the cloud never guessin'
while realizing it's a blessin'.
Wicked I was
Golden in sin
The choice never was
To be in the light that is thin
The dominance of Jesus Christ captured my path to be forgiven in
the wrath.

I'm a Christian

Walking with deniers
Cellular speaks Christian
In hell they are the fryers
Phone home is Christian
No sin is higher than the other
The king once said to another
Living with sinners
House shelter Christian
wicked cheating winners
Habitat is Christian,
Strength is prayer
Consciousness is preacher say'er
Until the time to arrive in Judgement and Jesus bares my sin, I'm a
Christian!

I Know of

The devil screams shut up!
In seeing the path of the return of Jesus Christ
Forgive the blind and give thanks to father for another healthy day
Forgive the wicked heist
Consciousness in father for the better day
The devil now knows the time
Equip with the blood of the king being prepared in his words of chime
While the devil tantrums with the angel hums.

Reflection

Wild adultery
Why have it been my place to live?
Now I see how lost it is
With no light to give
Still we all are his
Temple of the dog can't
Trample of the beast will
Better be a holy bible ant
Word of God prefill
Wild adultery
Have it ever went to ruins
How have I been so dark?
My spirit connected with hope as faith has it.
Still the enemy has it bark
So I'm glad I'm no wicked no more, having father to adore.

Pray pt. One

Praying is my thing
Gets my spirit to sing
Closeness to Creator
Now and later
The path to peace
As I once dangled close in being a monster
Having no attention to prayer
The bullet hits my head
From gun of the word of God.
I become a slayer
Stop the habit of sin in bed
Rest with the word of God
Praying is daily in I
Peaceful mind, Jesus Christ the invisible guy.
The power of God is to pray.

Sleepy sinner

Sleep sinner as angels guide you to your spirit that is with and of God
Sleep thinner, rest on cold rocks stones until you see to be and of God
Then realize the only sorrow is you are away from father
The highest dark rulers has ask forgiveness and has no way to bother
For they haven't stop sinning, so sleep sinner as angels guides you to your spirit that is with God.

The Highlight

Rise and shine
There something about the world
Oh it's the message of the second coming of Christ
Oh how prepared am I?
Am I doing my duty to pay the price
Away from sin is my passion till I die
The world alone sins and can't hide from the grave in the city
The world thrones sin and can't guide stubbornness of pity
Only God can do the ability of miracles
Oh, it's true the message of the second coming of Christ.

Early Death of Dad

Ever belief in God and died early?
It takes strong faith to make it true belief at the end
Bullets inside children
Disease stops your continuous life
Victim of murderous adrenaline
Never became long lived husband and wife
Have you ever belief in God and died early on your journey?
The strong faith that is made and felt before the end of flesh.

Red Riding Hood

What mighty words she speaks!
Settles me in the light inside the darkness
Kindles the flame of Jesus Christ
What lovely touch she has!
Soft and tender that gives satisfaction of living life
Bears the flame of Jesus Christ
Yet the feedback of her existence has a wolf on her trail, the very meet to sin and danger, I'm aware
She sways to me and asks, "How is the faith in believing there is God you have?"

Believable

How I know there is a God?

The gift of knowing a mother in my life, the shine of women to still be my wife,

How one does know?

Usually, it's automatic belief

His word does say bless are the ones believe without proof

To understand and comprehend that makes it believable there is a God.

I Pray

During nights, I pray for neighbor to be directed away from sin
Recurring sights, the wars and rumor of wars the sinful grin
I speak high as I ride high
The tweak of the wicked eye can lie
Still the Lord shields me in the dark
Next to sinners is where I park,
Faith in the Lord to appear
Give a sight that sin isn't near
Sanity from your word
Let it be in the jungle that's absurd
During nights, I pray for neighbor to be directed away from sin
Recurring lights, to give my hope to their shine and faith to their beam.

Like to Know

Never went to bible school
Departed from God since then
It was sin and my will to not be a sinner
Came the power of the invisible Creator
Sudden will power
World in better view
Consciousness at peace
Satisfactory in natural mystic
Glued to be a child of the creator post then.

From Stranger to Neighbor

Walking in the streets
Stranger gives me a hit of a joint
Faith in God in the sheets
Looking for a way, a point
Concrete wilderness
Nights thinking
Word of God tenderness
The north star blinking
Whispers of neighbor
As I stare at the thousands of people
Then form a prayer that is a flavor
To the enemy it's lethal
Packing years manifest
Tracking tears faithful with a chest
Walking in the streets
Once a neighbor gave me smoke from a joint.

Am to Be

In the dark I can't reside no longer
I need life, need to deal with the choices
Hurtful emotions influence sin
Having no care, be the first to dare
Give belief in the God to become stronger
Be faithful and restraint in the dark noises
The days of no evil behavioral actions makes the win
Have faith to bare, not to dare
In the light I'm to be, with forgiveness and strengthen faith in God
as I spree.

Pray pt. Two

I am satisfied by what I pray
No danger, wise choices,
positive stranger, silent rejoices,
Changing habit not to sin
Setting still for hours
Making the negative not win
Surrounding has the sours
Gateway
Leeway
Still, I strengthen the will
Not to fight fire with fire
No snowball rolling down the hill
Aim the light for its hire
I'm satisfied by what I pray.

Highlights

Rocky driveway
Grandfather says it's my way
Solider to the country, aware of the Lord.
Hold her to the country, where the law is Christ.
Red house, family irregular
Devil captures, darkness in the soul
Dead mouse, family regular
Sinner murders, child alone in whole
Grandfather silently direct
Bad habit tends to stop
From an awakening dialect
It's the lord's invisible power making you straight!

Faith to Dream

Slick n shine
What dreams are mine?
Dracula of light
My faith is your might
Is it my dreams as well
Only time will tell

Praise

Glory to God
For I'm seeing the blessing
Living with a gift of knowing a love one
Have been showed mercy to straighten my journey to the better-
ment then on
Glory to God
Adore what's seeing is the blessing
To comprehend the intellectual, know of the received sight of the
care from the power of the invisible God is the blessing
My hope is to be forgiven from his glory and enter the kingdom
Glory to God.

Love thy Enemy

Waiting to meet again
In clear smokeless
Yet sin is a natural habit
I know you will mean none of it when we meet again
Dear hopeless
It's my sight that gives in
Being faithful is a natural habit
I know you will not mean none of it when we meet again.

Inner Dream

The serpent is thrilled world peace can't happen
The amused keeps on clappin'
She awaits for me
To know her name
And let the love be
Still I walk away from the game
See she is everything
The gift from God
Yet I aim for more to make heaven sing
Be the gift from God
To damn the serpent and light the sinner into the delight King
And be in marriage alone in God.

His Sandals

Sandals of he
Leaves words I follow
Sight of sin brightful in the country
Was one in the dark country
Myself aim for forgiveness
As the habit of sin dissolves in me
With his core live this
The sandals of he
Leaves imprint of his words to follow.

The Notion

One, two, three, four
The king's blood is at the door
Ready to forgive when answered
Ready to wash away the bad, transferred
To be closer to the father in complete
To stop sinning before death is the goal to compete
One, two, three, four
Ready or not his blood been on the floor

Adultery

One time I think of her
Because she was for sale
Heart in the dirt
How can I prevail
Forgiveness does alert
Stands out in the junk mail
Read for read still I can see
Is it you or is it me?
Having search for something in pleasure
The quick shooting motion is the treasure
Adultery
Can never set you free
Normalize taste is disgrace
Forgiveness from his loving grace
Adultery
Will apart you to be
The lasting flame
Yet the rain will wet your fame.

The New World

Sin is sightful in the new world
Can touch the boy and touch the girl
And I'm the one that can see
Been in it chains
Thank God I'm free
Am in restraints
Can't think of sin
To do it again
As it shows in the norm in the new world.

Damn It

I'm not your sex buddy
I'm your conversation
Im not a winner or a loser
I don't play I actually live
He and she can be friendly
Am in glory of God when they are
I live in faith among the faithful
The silent light out in the loud dark
Can't be screaming for any complaints
Cause I see the horizon next to Jesus.

Moonlight Drive

She walks remembering her parents
He drives keeping his wife in memory
The young speeds their life
As the old lives in the young
Along the moonlight drive
Let's glow with the moon
Shine on oceans
Be close of God
The thing you see while activity partakes
Have stories with the knights of Jesus Christ
Be so loud in shine of partaking shape of the creator
Be in the backseat of the moonlight drive
Making it ours in our naked dances
Bright the areas to caress
While man connects to God in prayer
Along the moonlight drive.

Them Preachers

I believe them preachers in me
Live sin free among the king's throne
Some live on into the grave
Some need golden confirmation
Just behave as them preachers
Be inside alone in the king's throne
Give sight to humanity of the creator's law
I feel so satisfied figure it came from them preachers.

Automatic Faith

Calm during the storm
Peace comes living by father's law
The belief comes alive as long you believe
The dark is there to reject it through it all
Matureness righteous your strength of wise
Gather the information why you exist
The meaning why you are here won't come as a surprise
As the dark is loud believing in God is the twist.
Everything is alright without worry in knowing there is a Creator
that cares for its creation.

Aware

I greet sin early
Killer touch my dad
Wrongfully sexual advances
Consciousness depth in wicked
Always heard what the word of God said
Cornered, in cell the word of God enhances
Consciousness friendly Convo non-conflicted
Always forgiving God giving peaceful sleep in any bed
Memory of sin trances
Consciousness ends wrong habit, no flame on the flick end
I met sin early now I'm aware of the king's forgiveness.

What is Said

Happiness is a day without sin
Joy is the continuance days of no sin
Calm is forgiving the jerk
Stable is knowing how to pray in life's work
Satisfied is knowing your wise will cause no sin
Peace is natural habit to reject sin
The emotions written down by the religious clerk.

9 798869 347886